Sullen Weedy Lakes

Sullen Weedy Lakes

POEMS BY

William Logan

David R. Godine · Publisher

BOSTON

First published in 1988 by
David R. Godine, Publisher, Inc.
Horticultural Hall
300 Massachusetts Avenue
Boston, Massachusetts 02115

Library of Congress Cataloging in Publication Data
Logan, William, 1950–
Sullen weedy lakes.
I. Title.
PS3562.0449 S8 1988   811'.54   87-46289
ISBN 0-87923-729-5
ISBN 0-87923-730-9 (soft)

First Edition
Printed in the United States of America

Acknowledgment is owed to the editors of the magazines which first printed some of these poems:

Agni Review: The Air of Cathedrals; Ambassador of Imperfect Mood; Anglian Music; Babies; *Un Nocturne Révolutionnaire*; The Rivers of England. *Crazyhorse*: Racial Prejudice in Imperial Rome. *Critical Quarterly*: Chiaroscuro; Debora Sleeping. *Denver Quarterly*: Banana Republics; California from England; The Inns and Outs of Irony; Propriety. *Grand Street*: Coleridge in the Hurricane; Moorhen; On the Late Murders; Political Song. *Harvard Magazine*: Religious Kindling. *The New Criterion*: To the Honourable Committee. *The New Yorker*: The North Atlantic; The Virus in Rude Weather. *Paris Review*: August in the Straits; The Duck Pond; Haddocks' Eyes; The Imitative Fallacy. *Sewanee Review*: Convention of Liars; Elms and Antiques; Major Graves; The New World. *Shenandoah*: Auden; Darwin in the Ditch; The English Museum; The Great Wildlife of the Church. *Southwest Review*: The Ancient Economy. *Yale Review*: Capability Brown in the Tropics; Disease and Etiquette.

"James at Sixty" appeared in *For James Merrill: A Birthday Tribute* (Jordan Davies, 1986), edited by J.D. McClatchy. "Shakespeare and Science" was written for a conference on "Shakespeare's Personality" at the University of Florida in 1985. "Political Song" was reprinted in *Harper's*.

The poems in the first part of this book were published, some for the first time, in *Moorhen* (Abattoir Editions, 1984). The author is grateful to Harry Duncan for his kindness.

These poems could not have been written without the aid of an Amy Lowell Poetry Traveling Scholarship and a grant from the National Endowment for the Arts. The University of Florida generously provided two research grants, and a leave of absence during which the work was completed.

for James Merrill and Donald Justice

Contents

When I must shipwrack, I would do it in a Sea,
where mine impotencie might have some excuse;
not in a sullen weedy lake, where I could not have
so much as exercise for my swimming.

John Donne

Sullen Weedy Lakes

Moorhen

To have
red mouth and green shanks
    like a sidewalk hooker
come up through the ranks
    of weeds does not disqualify
you from honorary membership
    in the upper class,
the community of spies,
    or any lowly clan
not put off by outer feathers that
    conceal the inward man.

    Or hen in this case, unsexed
like Lady Macbeth or the Chairs;
    though no more rude than the next
species downstream
    you've never grown fat
like a capon on chocolate éclairs.
    The dictionary calls you
a *common* gallinule,
    an insult, I suppose.
Your family has elongated
    webless toes,

    but all families have problems,
marital or genetic,
    in search of a mastering art
or a convenient aesthetic.
    Admiral, it's an admirable life
asleep on the water
    above crepuscular plants
and miniature pike
    that never need to be tended

and never go out on strike.
        You nose among the rank

        roots, washed white and ghostly,
grasses weave on the bank,
        where bugs, I assume, have costly
apartments, and are always behind with the rent.
        And you, you're the rent collector,
dealing in first-born sons
        and daughters, grannies, long-lost cousins,
virtually everyone.
        How convenient to be a ridiculous
rapacious insectivore,
        much better than being dependent

        on a grocery store.
How convenient to maintain a demeanor:
        when chased or thwarted by fear
you sail between the weeds
        and disappear.
Did you descend from the moors,
        purple and lush with heather,
far away from the stores
        and with indifferent weather?
Better here in the lowlands
        full of *noblesse oblige;*

        where the rats own baby grands
Inland Revenue never lays siege.
        Reduced to one expression,
call it amused but grave,
        that achieves its own lesson

on the etiquette of where to behave,
        you plod with unwieldy grace
as if the ditch were a minefield
        and not a froth of lace.
I feel estranged
        that way too, sometimes—we all do, hen,

        but what's the use?
You'll wake tomorrow and the ditch
        will not have changed.

Auden

Untrue to the spirit if not the letter of love
he descended from passes to domestic grandeur
where railway carriage halting at checkpoint
as likely betrayed actor, vicar, or out-of-work spy.
Why not by being false be true to a people
whose glaciers control not valleys but blood?
What worries the widows weakens the warriors,
bothers the breeders, damns the departments.

When schemes of architecture scaled the island
the pale clerks plotted to ransack his estates,
supposing by absolving the present of error
errors past might for the month be dishonored.
In the weakening city who can forgive
the suffering valley's thirst for alcohol?
What deranges the drivers drowns the delayers,
perils the prudent, errors the engines.

The harvest of teacups commemorates the slaughter
of knives and forks, the treaty of tablecloth.
A healing moment starts the silence of accusal:
Can his correctible beauty betray
a body's corruptive imprisonment, a throat
constricting on the appalling perfume?
What collapses the climbers clouds the computers,
surrounds the survivors, lures the lovers.

The Inns and Outs of Irony

Blue as a wound beneath skin, light
bears these bruised messages from the field:

June in England, unseasoned heats thin
the armor of a love, or love congealed.
Our time hammers words we dare not vary,
as if desire had monstered to embarrassment

our bodies' common circumstance. Wary
gesture, not the Gallic prisoner consent,
defrays the language that betrays us. We romance
to think ourselves shackled, not privileged.

All Britain this hospital between the ants
and what scavenges after, vulture blood fledged
with lies, light—lab where the dusty wish
of culture cultures the dawn in its dish.

Anglian Music

The flint church in the market square
grounds the worked-out pits
where Neolithic diggers scrounged
the chalk with antler picks.

The iron summer's cold clouds shake
a hail that bludgeons fields of corn,
then rattles in windrows, stone
cracked along a reedy beach:

its scythe will break the flail.
This season the round God barks
through His rose window, and oak pews
clot the stream of foreign visitors

who tweak the nose of our unnamed local knight
and muzzle his sleeping dog. When Cromwell
thieved the brass from our Crusader
and pounded to gristle his marble brains,

our narrow churchman cowered in the crypt.
Darkness bladed his ax. He crept out to slay
the minions low along the wall,
and stumbled in the butchered clock among the stones.

There spreads the sheepish lichen still called blood.
We sweat beneath the new Protectorate
whose Lady's thirst drinks up our state.
The fishermen with maggots in their mouths

await the revolution of the trout,
and pregnant school-leavers roll like tanks

their bulky prams along crazed walks.
No devil in the gloom catches grazing horses

by the throat, but down the smoking river
blind mist rootles poisoned wildflowers
and bindweed shocks the summer grass.
I wait beside the lone elm

bending its arthritic limb against itself.
Along the bark a sparrow sharps its bill.
A threatening snail, its horns erect,
slides up the damp wall like an unrigged ship.

The Air of Cathedrals

The starling perched in winter's spackled plumage
bothers bleached lawns. The bramble thorn, the holly,
razors of a privileged nature protect

the skirmishes of intellect. Color or color's lack:
gaudy painted cathedrals scraped down
to gray stonework, the friendly chill of the tomb.

These, and vines and ivies hacked at root
to bare the modern taste for clean line.
Or not intellect, but the final days of grace

in masquerade. From marble tombs with false noses
all rise up with rheumatism at Judgment;
but the punk's pink Mohawk spikes

steal neither face nor false passion,
the trendy rage no less impotent or beautiful for that.
The seasons, like monarchists, pretend to succession;

spring's morose crowning, apple blossoms
blazing like fireworks,
today's cut daffs next week's old lace,

leaving even to dead elms their magnificent empty space.
Like the monks they have replaced,
moorhens stalk the university's plucked grounds.

Ely's lopsided cathedral, rising like Mothra
from the fens it has laid waste,
stretched on Roman drains to the sea

where waves like fen tigers still pronounce
th as *f*, inbreeds these minor, elegant histories
with landscape. The marshes where Hereward

held off until betrayed the bloody Normans
now yearly sink toward unreachable bedrock,
collapsing into themselves like a dead star

whose placid farmers crop its fertile surface.
The Norman tower's now clunch rubble,
each tribe building on a tribe's tawdry weight,

crushing mercenary villa, priory,
and soon the council estates.
Dredges hourly bare a manmade Celtic island

a hundred yards from the old shore—
timbered down to gravel, watery fortress
against the bureaucratic Angles or a raft

for keeping Celtic feet out of water.
Drained, the marshes foster viruses
that strip a man down to skeleton, like piranhas.

The ribbed stonework
rots the land no revelation dares emigrate.
Some drains have Roman ancestry, some empires.

Capability Brown in the Tropics

Even if evening elected a lover
from countless candidates, the mountain would murmur
against such devices derived from textbooks.
The ordinary architect achieves order
by renting remission to rare fevers,
his plaster walls washed with coral,
a pink imputation, purely informal,
like a greeting to guests, late or unwanted.
His ponds lie open to arrangements of carp,
his muted mathematics nearly a nature
examined by x-ray. Such fish expect no one.
Elsewhere lakes languish, luring to shore
unrepentant anhingas, their oilless wings
spread like the fans of infamous geishas.

The Barbarian Sack of Rome

The dovecot poisons the dove.
First is the shift of warning,
neither hereditary
nor so communicable

as to frighten the neighbors
or scare off cheap physicians.
Lizards disconcert the screens;
blood-orange, mephitic sunsets

will tilt the low horizon.
What circumstances apply
have rarely applied before.
The weather of monarchies,

whose fungal lineages
answer with a false decor,
is used to ordinary
diplomacies, as no true

science can promise or bear.
The skin may be mastered now
by new effusions of frost,
or such gorgeous ripe flushes

as bother the late apples
and the brilliant engorged moon,
once so psychoanalyzed.
The lowly bear the city

away on their backs, and dogs
explore the entrails of dogs.
In the privileged sectors
the shaken heights of the rose

would argue a misfortune.
Still there is time to prepare
a hotel for banished kings
humored by pastel stamps

overprinted with new names.

Darwin in the Ditch

The mutant ducklings gliding through ditches,
whose parents feather cobalt salts,
copper alloys, bronze oxidating to verdigris,

now gear backward mastering forward motion.
Thin rats steal down from the cow parsley
to gnaw the young for their young.

If Darwin is God, Darwin is a cruel god,
bespectacled form dispassionately observing
the orange underlighting of apartment windows,

whose mocking shadows simplify desire
to a few Platonic shows on off-white walls,
hereditary lusts or indiscreet affairs—

poor steel engravings to a lover,
or would-be lover, in her underwear.
Beyond the weedy DNA's choking the ditch,

which runs with metaphor from mysterious source
to gothic outlet, stocked fish hesitate
at banked shadows and the grass

leering from the stilted moorhen's nest
into water whose decay refracts.
Their slit bellies moon the grasses'

silver undersides, folding over when
simplicity arranges gravity's argument.
There are always beauties to distract from blood.

The Rivers of England

How we too shoulder arrogance, weapon
of the poor against the poor: our guttering
litanies sung to these arguments.
Gill-netted fish, tubercular badger,

poisoned swan ghosting through bare waters toward
shires flaked of steel and coal.
Asian ports now control the fire before the hob,

the glass toy-theater whose puppets glaze
polished boards. The kestrel's silence, the crow's
triumphal caw, the kingfisher perched above streams

like a judge over sentences within—

to pluck one out, and make it rhyme with law—
return where water fails to flow from maps:
strikes have hammered shut the rusted taps.

The New World

Rusted insects with rust wings beat
the crumbled mortar where they sun.
Out of ripening summer, their immunities

repay the temperate rankness of the lawn.
How earn from this world miraculous forebears,
the sown world rising, crops they lopped

carelessly, like the heads of lords?
The sharpened stake of reason
nudges the nose with odors of human meat.

And still occasion surfaces, like algae
on the lake, summoning even from the hearts
of exiles some abraded memory of home,

its splendid participles, aged nouns,
sinuous, dusty verbs communicating
snow-choked headlands with rebellious plains.

Beneath the alien banner of this weather,
fens extend where swallows float and dart
and whip the air for black-headed flies

tonguing their meal and maggot.
Grant, then, their secular fallacies,
sea monsters whose discoveries turned upon themselves.

From their voyages what tobaccos and taboos.

August in the Straits

The great blue heron's tinctured swerve
fires its yellow bill with the trout's alloy.
Why in place of nature cure

a fluency that betrays the tongued
compartments of the phonograph?
Year after year the white oaks

open to the gaze of passersby,
ibis, stork, and crane sharing
the half-light of stalls

and center aisles of their immunity.
These theatrical arrangements aggravate
the loss and literature of their climate,

the slash and burn that serve
as *aide-mémoire* to the general text.
They contemplate strange alphabets, the dead,

limbs locked in politics of disbelief.
The coinage of their argument
choirs Roman marble in spotless halls,

the crow perched on the emerald Augustus.
Memoirs of empire, whose sharpened teeth
still coral the beaches. Even the echoes

rearranging the plotters' camp
keep meters of the tidal shore, and long past darkness
the coast lights vibrate

toward offshore boats, floating like unpaid legions.
Against them, a mercenary breeze
whose pale moths wing like olive leaves.

The North Atlantic

I

Days it lorded above us like a coin,
days the white sun gave what we purloined.
I slept with one hand on the bunk's steel frame
and one beneath the pillow, gripping for luck
a scalloped Kodak. The lemons lasted
almost till Iceland, the gin hardly a suck.
Old Smith, our bootlegger, soon dismasted,
could bribe in Russian. It was a wartime game,
like poker under Scarne's rules, or craps
in the naval barracks after taps.
The bottles bobbed in our wake like corks.
They swim forth now in fishy shoals,
the memories in tan and cream, snow and coals,
like the oily winters of New York.
Postwar, post-discharge, when color came,
nothing fixed, in the black leather books,
shots in avalanche like shale, shots of cooks,
maids, discarded afternoons lurching into focus,
gliding back into favor though all in frame
had lost their heads. One's in Caracas,
one's dead, most have lost their names.
Garden party, wedding reception, wake?
On long tables the Mouton-Rothschild fakes
a tipsy siesta. No argument trammels
the folding chairs. Here we ate our dead,
the prawns. The summer boys, who begged their Camels,
would fight like Spartans when the world
saw sailors drown like rabbits at the Pearl.
We cargoed Iceland's frozen mail, instead—
shadowed convoys, gambled, listened for the U-
boats, but mostly ran the sacks of mail,

dropping charges when a sperm or blue
troubled the sonar, and left a bloody whale.
One snowy morning slicks broke on the sea
behind us, boiling to the surface like a stew.
In them, life jackets and garbage. Debris.
The black cooks promised us our share of slaughter.

· II ·

Dry land unseasons bodies, broken down
with arrowpoints and shattered pots in shallow ground,
but the sea takes any trepanned skull
and makes it home. Shining ribs, coralled bone,
cage for the tiger fish, for the crab a hull—
brittle Tiffany for undersea empires.
The octopus is lord among the stones.
His sedimented ships are spires.
One night a torpedoed tanker leaked its crude
on the flat sea, burning, the flames like lace.
They could not launch rafts, the men on deck.
The sailors shivered in that latitude,
hunching as the black tanker groaned within—
steel plate blistering from the fire inside,
paint down the superstructure sloughing like skin—
and slowly, and not so silently, fried.

Babies

· I ·

The apple shaved of blossom feeds on May.
If the sun, darkening an intransigent clearness,
sharpens rough blades on rough blades,

the body, fattening, becomes the only subject
the eye withholds from. My distant sister,
to almost everyone of your sex comes

unhappy ripening.
What harms in love is love's intemperate
exhaustion of the physical, using us

up like spiders that egg and die.
Fantasies on which we feed tell us
our miniature replacements improve

by their presence, draw blood by absence.
Who can answer criticisms not of conscience
but convenience? Those who live satisfied

with brutalities of scale, distant
from skirmishes that leave real dead,
answer for no one. Light-blind moths

into daylight fan the glass they cannot enter.
The mallard in the pane
herds the starving ducklings against the river.

II

For casual artifacts we try to be good.
For patchwork quilts, sloughing in generous
leaves their diseased skin, we try to observe,

though in that country
chalk madonnas rainbow the walks,
syphilitic lions prowl rank gardens.

From muds in featureless streams,
the thieving kingfisher climbs the arc of air
with its throbbing trout.

On tin-roofed streets, *campesinos* bleed
through white shirts whose history must be abstract.
The steaming walks crowd with women,

skirts full of black-market transistor radios.
After rain gutters the blood,
the palms like looms shuttle their warnings,

weaving back and forth in the clotted air.
That is the horror, not to be style any longer—
skeleton starving posterity's anatomist

where knowing is acted in each unknowing.
Here, men tether their children, and even women
are only men with large chests and flat genitals.

Banana Republics

Gone now, the remarkable harvests
when machete scraped back jungle to reveal
the mossy temple, by next season
frondy undergrowth again. The mothy breathing
of money in foreign capitals, inhaling
its increase, weaves around the paddleboats
sunk at docks, spent mansions
beside the earth-colored river
where a chair floats upside down, its caned back
netting crimson fish threading upstream,
all four legs rising above the swell
like a snail's waving horns or the drawn swords
on bronze statues of corroded revolutionaries.

Through an open window, night's membrane rests
on a gilt frame where seagulls
turn across a dull oil of sky,
Holsteins browse burnt-umber hills, and the shepherd
swerves his crook against the bready sheep,
loaves for the wolf that slinks against the copse—
or only a sheepdog wronged by veneer,
all to resurrect, above Mozart's snowy slopes,
some species of return where now
the lordly cockroach trembles and stills,
overseeing its domain. A night bird cries.
The lizard on the wall uncurls its tongue
around a fly. The ceiling fan revolves,
a ship propeller turning thickly
through rafts of seaweed; and green moonlight—
as if the moon *were* cheese—immerses the lizard,
the cockroach, the piano in the vast private bay
where marijuana sloops cast off toward customs
of a common shore. Kind Jorge, late of the bar

in the Hotel de la Revolución, now cradles
his Kalashnikov on a back seat, awaiting the Guardia.
The capitalistic children ask to shine his shoes.

Memoirs of Empire

I · PROPRIETY

Every exile becomes his own early corpse,
having faced those indrawn to their homes
like great pistons plunging their limited confines.

No metaphor dragged from rain can be drowned there.
The long river falls vertically
from sheep ditch and fen drain, arteries

drawing to conclusion the muddied instances
a pleasing constancy appeals to. All exile
is withholding, finding in alien landscape

a personal swerve. The traitorous swallows
whose fierce blood chafed the common
have flung themselves on helpless insects

in Africa. The Empire's boats steam home,
full of zinc-lined coffins, bodies torn
from the rainy muck of helpless islands.

We prey on one another, and if the man,
his dark lungs sweetening, succumbs
to the length of occasion—no longer arrowed

like a weather vane toward home—he will awake
to his body stopped with wax and cord.
Those who do not learn the lessons of the future

are doomed to repeat it.

The kingfisher's hot-rod blue body
arrows to a trout nosing its dry aquarium,
a politician wired in his humility.

We too enter honesty like a grave,
exhibit for what generations come,
palms to the glass, to tender their observations:

glazed panes oversee the cathedral city
now more secular than cobblestone or market garden.
God in period costume coughs in panic's dry fashion.

Everywhere the past contents its glass cabinets:
the guest brushes away dust to find
a miniature light tearing at housetops,

storm's flash and tear cutting the weir
where plates of smashed rock slip and scare
swans bellying to the bank. Beneath marble's

lit addresses, the storm's wash eddies
toward the vortex of the lamp, drawn
like pale, luxuriant moths.

In the next case, Napoleon's sailors,
far from their *vin ordinaire*,
carve bone guillotines for the prison tourist.

Not one escapes the prison of his desire.

Elms and Antiques

The harsher shores establishing our rites
are pastel boundaries, skins estranging
the traveler from customs sheds he has been waved through,

the sandy spits breached by tar
and the horizon's closure, false weather
fogging the mainland wharves and their insignificant

ballasts. Like quill pens the spars
rise above the mist, and oyster shells chasten the asphalt,
such comprehending images for the photograph

that in a frame converts the gassed bodies
of General Motors to Jews. Our diseases
complete their vocations, their passages,

by manning innocents of labor, the mass
shuffling at docks their sepia clothing,
facing out to sepia oceans.

Picture them, lost forebears clutching
cardboard valises, like the guerrillas
forced through streets with their Samsonite.

Debora Sleeping

The ferry window frames a pop-art shovel,
jaw drooling gouts of water and harbor mud.
The drawn-in gangplank scrapes against the wood.
A few shy children pelt the boat with gravel,

but the stones fall short. The boat's an oven.
Outside the seagulls circle, lazy and overweight,
crying against decisions of the state
like wingèd burghers stacked up outside heaven.

The French and Spanish ports decline midway
between bureaucracy and art, but while
waiting for the Fifties to return to style
they condescend to watch our nights and days.

You're asleep again, as on the leaf-lit train,
though here a purple plastic chair's your bed.
The pre-Raphaelitic curls that wreathe your head
are permanent—at least, immune to rain,

unlike the satin shirt I made you wear
in Paris, that did not outlast the storm.
You spent the evening huddling to keep warm
and whispered phrase–book curses in my ear.

Sleep's our disease, the heart's adagio.
We wallow in its sty, refuse to leave
the rundown precinct of its raveled sleeve,
the only ease bodies so close can know.

Or so I thought. Watching you here
sleep in hard daylight—hulled on that dream beach,

drugged (courtesy Dramamine), silent, out of reach—
I know the first stirring of a distant fear.

The boat wakes toward chalk cliffs closed by fog
where fishermen not out of work still bear
the dying and disputed catch ashore.
Sleep by other means continues dialogue.

Christ Church, Oxford / 26 October 1881

My dear little girl,

    (There! I don't think I ever began
a letter like that before—in all my life.
    But of course I shall soon have
to alter it: you see our friendship began

    so *awfully* quick—quite dangerous,
it was so sudden—almost like a railway-
    accident: that it's pretty
sure to end off just as suddenly. Next year,

    we shall have got to shaking-hands terms,
and the year after we'll be on bowing terms,
    just when we happen to see
each other at opposite sides of the street.)

    Please do not think I am beginning
to forget you, because I am so lazy
    about writing: but oh! oh!
I'm so *awfully* busy! What with teaching,

    looking over answers to questions,
and writing lecture-business, and these letters,
    sometimes I get *that* confused,
I don't know which is me and which the inkstand.

    Pity me, Marion, my dear child!
The confusion in one's *mind* doesn't so much
    matter—but when it comes to
putting bread-and-butter, and orange marmalade,

into the *inkstand*; then dipping pens
into *oneself*, and filling *oneself* with ink,
   it is *awfully* horrid!
One of my pupils this term is a negro,

   with a small face as black as a coal,
and frizzly wool for hair. I have had to keep
   a label on the skuttle,
and a label on him, marked in large letters,

   in black ink, "THIS IS THE COAL-SKUTTLE"
and "THIS IS HIM," so as to know which is which.
   Many thanks to your mother
for her letter, and I'll write to her some *year*.

   Always your loving friend,
   C. L. Dodgson

3–13 *September 1752*

And what an indulgence is here, for those who
love their pillow to lie down in Peace
on the second of this month and not perhaps
awake till the morning of the fourteenth.
From every autumn there is an absence,
a marriage of need to Georgian necessity,
the walnut table abandoning its leaves
like the oaks theirs.
                              Such compromise
still panels an ardor with royal circumstance,
such partial and implied powers as could not stop
the planets in their orbits to illustrate a dogma.
Cholera among the farmers, the lords
muffled in their chambers, a sudden fall
shortened in its count, to whose advantage
other than the diplomats' do the yoked weeks
cooperate?
                    And like unruly hedges, hallowing
the rumpled thrushes on their nests, the year
needs pruning. And like the badger, savaged
in its sett, it shrinks a little to survive.
An act fillets its circumstance, and king and lord
will follow Christ's vicar to a settlement
with Caesar, yanked like a fish from the bloody womb.
The sceptre *that* bent out of true, the deaf
will introduce a motion to implicate the hearing.
Even in minor histories some days have never
deserved to exist. On Thursday awakens the laborer,
two weeks' wages lost, the sun still in the sky,
all lives whittled by Parliament, the month
collapsed like Hogarth's drunkard, trampling on the flag
embroidered, "Give us our eleven days."

California from England

The pastel Ovid, limping toward Rome to find
the scrolls remaindered, the lover in a new

X-rated number, and even the emperor
no longer dispensing the physic of his anger,

pleads for lost worlds with the etiquette of strangers.
Returning can never recover a luster,

oyster-lit hills competing with sunset
or sad crowds of palms razoring noon air.

Dreams in the rough sleep of exile
are clawed by foreign rooks, infections

like accent or pale stamps
defaced with the queen's young profile.

Ignorance itches worse than betrayal.
The traveler is absent from all lands equally,

discovering only scenes unequal to his necessity:
the seals we heard inhabited the rocks that,

for us, were barren.

The Underground

The hollow light of London, late afternoon,
filters through the main bank's central hall,
the paneled chamber that shadows upward toward
the unwashed skylights of a Moorish dome
where mottled pigeons on autumn evenings flutter,
trapped against the glass, descending by stages
to alight beside a feverish clerk's accounts
whose ledger of foreign exchange is told and tilled
as city churches toll the landlocked hour.
Beyond brass grilles by mahogany railings stand
sallow representatives of the *beau monde*
waiting for bills to clear the manicured fingers
of clerks who turn from signatures to stare
at the slight constructive shudder in the walls,
shivering dust from the breasts of wooden nymphs
and the fruit they lie on, and launching chalky powder
down upon silk hats, through cones of gaslight
spilling from green shades onto the baizes'
pale green fields, in mock reminder of
the partner's blown glass globe that hurls its flakes
of snowdrift upward from the ground, to settle
carelessly upon the skaters painted
in frozen passion on a mirrored rink.
Cigar smoke binds the oak Corinthian pillars
like wild grapes etched within the precincts of
the Coliseum by the *émigré* engraver,
fingers stained with nicotine, who peers across
the low spiked wicket toward the senior clerk.
The floury ash sifts down upon his shoulders.
The milk-faced gentlemen soberly discuss
news from the Crimea, a decline in stocks.

The clerk still scolds his miserable apprentice,
whose hat that noon, toppled by an errant cane,
scattered the canvas reticule of notes
entrusted there, and on the wind dispensed
old money to the crowd of accident.

II · THE CAKE OF CUSTOM, 1914

And what is mastered by the master's pawn?
A gentleman lifts his silver-headed cane
to probe a shattered window, while blasts of snow
ferret beneath the iron overhang
and drift in dunes across his boots. The cane knop,
worked into a monkey's grinning skull,
warms its chattering teeth within his hand.
Down the alley come the screams of pigs.
Leaning on his cane, he takes the gale
windward between two buildings, his glass eye
hollowed out with cold, or memory of cold.
He enters the abattoir, and cracks the cane against
the Georgian writing desk three pigs' heads bleed on.
Their candied faces repay the mirrored glazes
of the walnut burl. Two steaming butchers turn.
One wraps a bloody hand around a beer.
Remember still the sainted name of Morphy.
That gentleman lights an antique carriage lamp
and with the cane descends the spiral staircase
curving out of view, its broken steps
patched with scraps of lumber, moist walls lined
with peeling bills of fare, the ornamental
menus of a social class that once
found secret entrance to its restaurants.

The paneled door he unlocks opens on
Remember still the sainted name of Morphy
who strode the checkered squares in moleskin pants.
a circular ballroom lined with cabinets.
His lamp sets fire to the icy shards of glass
melting at his approach, and burns the sconces
tilting gas lamps from the mirrored walls.
Against the mirrors heaps of chairs and tables
protrude from rotting sheets, a dusty range
of *papier-mâché* mountains constructed for
the Balkan comedy abandoned till
the hills began their languid avalanche.

III · BALACLAVA C.I.F. LONDON, 1854

O take the dead where merchants cannot find
the sunken graves that would offend, offend.
The roll-top warren of pigeon holes contains
among raw bills of exchange, overripe accounts,
letters wreathed in circles of red tape,
among all these, two tickets to an opera.
From his inside pocket the *émigré* withdraws
the loose sheaf of a folded manuscript.
The clerk accepts it with a condescension
required by the manners of the house,
and if the quill that feathers his right ear
quivers with a confidential tremor,
his eyes betray no human interest.
The odor of stale perfume wads his nose,
but with a shy conspiring air he bends
examining the Russian manuscript.
He moves his lips in negligent perusal,

then slides the sheets into a lower drawer,
as if to shield from any observation
the moral opportunities war describes,
the flowers, hothouse fruit, and vintage wine
hoisted to the ships and gaily spread
(*O take the dead far hence, at our expense*)
through officers' cabins, all paying for
a war that purges from the country seats
utilitarian trust that bore the strike
of Preston spinners, Sheffield engineers,
or lack of Miniés, medicine, and tents.
Beneath the gibbet, dear, we walked a year,
then south to the cold stewed Indian tea.

IV · ROTHSCHILD'S PIGEONS, 1914

The governments sour like vintages of wine.
A ruined printing press subsides beneath
riggings of dust the gangs of spiders wove,
and in one cabinet the forgeries,
long out of date, tilt in dusty thousands
the bank notes' copperplate. The revolution
honors our failure in its execution:
the dream of 1848 now stains
the weathered stone of Highgate. The chiseled markers
freeze and crack until they slant like rooftops,
like the geometric problems of parquet
where here and there a crowbar has removed
floor and underfloor, the city's swollen river
bricked and boarded over, a black canal
that threads beneath the ordnance map and flushes
its deep sewers to the Thames. I've traced

its late meanders in the dust, as if
the polished course of history consecrates
those passages it passes by, those streets
that Parliament negates, or misremembers.
Gone, the railway mania, the alley
where little-go men fingered muddy letters,
ragged shawls selling their silent lights,
the Creole flower girl, the Irish beggar
wheeling along on his low wooden carriage,
porters in bottle-green coats, the beehive stove
beneath the crown of the dome, and clean-shaven clerks.
All these things seen and unsaid, said and unseen,
the pigeons conned each noon in Finsbury,
a lunch wrapped in a towel to keep it moist,
partners hobbling by in breech and stocking,
outdated as their grandfathers. The pride that fed
the old dispute about the keys now feeds
new trenches in the north of France, and Christ
whose feet were splayed, or nailed with one forged nail,
now violates the truce of dialects.
And No, No, I've never met, I've never met
The man from Alabammy that I couldn't forget.
The dead go squealing to their muddy graves
like music-hall comedians, or slaves.
The groan of pigs from upstairs orchestrates
the lighting of the lamps. Their mantles play
charades upon the ceiling, smoking corpses
repairing plaster wreaths and gilt medallions
now swept in parapets along the parquet,
greasy with the ink of blood. The monkey
absently investigates a bunch
of shattered grapes that crowns these ornaments.

V · THE STANDARD ASSASSIN, 1854

Shadowed by buildings whose new addresses
control the hour it now records in miniature,
the church clock visible down the narrow street
chimes faintly to the tune of Wren's design.
Out of his hansom cab a cheesy young man
knocks country mud from his boots, and purchases
a *Standard* from the blind newsboy who thumbs
shillings, pence, and farthings to separate pockets.
Within the deepening shade of brass-knobbed doors
he wraps his greatcoat over a revolver
as a waiter lays a napkin on his arm,
walks stiffly to the nearest cashier's desk,
then with the *Standard* tips the ink pot over,
and as the starched cashier extends his hand
to stop the welling ink, the pale assassin
shoots him in the eye. A porter shouts.
The *émigré* and senior clerk look up,
and when the first removes his spectacles
a vial of acid is flung into his face.
I plunge into the busy crowd, to rue;
They know me still the same, to rue, to rue;
And his smile was unalter'd, rue, to rue.

VI · BLUEBOTTLES, 1914

Summers when the flies, so ravenous
they clogged the ink pots on the windowsill,
mated on the air of the Thames, their Parliament
closed its windows to the smell and then
abandoned government for country house.

40

Decay attends decay, in measure of
the rising damp, the fall of soot from plaster.
The river's course work cuts its teeth on mortar,
descends on Roman tiles to the drains.
The gaslight flickered, and as I drew the cape
around me twice, the long-expected ghost
refused to rise. From cabinets I swept
the foreign bank notes with my simian cane,
clandestine knowledge sickening to the fabric
of an English gentleman, however ancient
or disposed against the kiss of government.
And such have I become. That gentleman was myself.
There are no longer any who remember
our cold conspiracies, the Tsar's machine
hurling acid and revenge, an eye blown out
by a spy's defective cartridge, and better lost
than forced to witness every further loss
the tenors of this century have sung,
the English armies wheeling toward the Somme.
The threats of youth are lost in youth, and what
the anarchies of foreign war produced
produces schemes of revolution in
a sailor's packet. I've sent a million rubles
over the black edge. I've risen to the stairs
to gather from my friends an unwashed ham.

Racial Prejudice in Imperial Rome

Tamquam scopulum, sic fugias inauditum
atque insolens verbum

Change resolves the landscapes
to the duties of mutual subjection,
gulls beating into the wind,

motionless against hornbeam and ash.
These histories approximate the language of the human
until corruption works upon them,

Livy's strutting Gaul, whooping before the tiny Roman,
dispatched with two short thrusts of the short sword.
The outward arts that inward motions fail

fail the razored dossiers crumpled in cabinets,
the hungers that are not the case, the specimens
some view as training, some terrain.

Consider the grebe's forgiveness, the mocking
of the gargoyle, each arrogating in stone
the meticulous skeins of conspiracy.

To such redeemers tender no contrivance or control.
The heron walks its shadow, the egret its intents,
and our own abrasive elsewhere avoids

the strange and unfamiliar word like a dangerous reef.
The mullet float on the lake like fans,
the lakes like blue fans.

Coleridge in the Hurricane

Two boats on a painted ocean do not prove
the mirror of nature controls the glass of art
until one boat or the other starts to move.
The Gulf Stream slowly forces boats apart

though neither boat may be inclined to move.
To anchor in the eye needs more than art,
it needs a crew whose motions will approve
yet stem the forces forcing boats apart.

Since no mind dulled with opium improves
before the damp addictiveness departs,
the hurricane will not be forced to move
Coleridge's nature, though it inform his art

that form is spirit. The spiral cannot move
the wretched mariner to play the part
that asks his drifting conscience to reprove
the murdered albatross that murders art.

Convention of Liars

There is no need, liars, to invoke
the paradox of Sumatra, where two tribes coexist
though one cannot learn to carve the lies
the other has come to measure truth by.

Though Conrad's sailors construe the horizon
as a national morality, the barometer's silver vein
foretells the spiral depletions of the typhoon.
Where the lay of the land lies in water,

intimate deceptions are required to traverse
islands whose pink shades do not show
a cartographer's duty to the crudely physical.
Lies are partial music, as their composers know:

the clippers tacking around strange landfalls
defraud only invoice and log,
the rosary of ports carrying forward
a system of accounts. Commend these statements

to wooden cabinets where nothing will question
their devious appointments, the ledgered diversions
whose remainders rot in tin-sheeted warehouses.
Prison colonies burn into the rain forest,

as if where empire legislates mahogany,
it legislates the watered gin of tropical spas.
Storms will bring in their rough voyage
what trade even insurance companies,

lodged in their London hotels, prefer to mark
in the balance sheets, not the mainsails.
To their drowned origin cannot be assigned
the expenditure of trust required.

The navigation chart will fail to note
where with precision the ship disappears
into the horizon, what consequence its absence entails,
where the wool-jacketed mourners vanish ashore.

Major Graves

On Wednesday mornings Major Graves would walk
around his island by ten o'clock,
brushing with his cane the hair of the natives
and plucking from bushes a raw sedative.

His descendants could not trace the harsh
tracks of his leather boots in the marsh,
though the precipitous decline in alligators
began in his refrigerator.

Every island has its green
regard for vagaries of scene
but Major Graves could not be held
to responsibilities of the veldt.

The mating cries of the quadrupeds
echoed in his great bald head,
but the notorious volume on wildlife
by rumor began with his wife.

The bitterberry provided ink
for tattoos and fermented drink.
Evenings the Major embellished his arms
with fauna and maps of his farm.

In months without *r* the absence of storms
permitted arrival of crates of forms
whose small print the natives took to be seed.
Their exports consisted of weed.

Their priests believed that to burn or freeze
was the manifestation of one disease.
After seven years they erected a god
shorter than he was broad.

Recalled to Whitehall by the Foreign Office
the Major contracted a jaundice.
He survived the fever but soon succumbed
to a gross infection of the gums.

His wrought-iron balcony from Savannah
supported a legislature of iguanas,
while ornate lamps perched on cupidons
let the dead with the living look on.

Un Nocturne Révolutionnaire

On the island of skeletons
a rusting fleet of freighters
indulged the mottled dictator's
ruinous passion for guns.

He wept on his marble throne
while journalists bled into pails
in the cells of art deco jails
built with agricultural loans.

He strangled the Catholic clerics,
set fire to books with a phrase,
but when he desired praise
he tortured his poets for lyrics.

The moon rose over the palace,
white as a wedding cake,
and burned down into the lake,
thin as a lethal bacillus.

All night the champagne flowered
in the government's thin-stemmed glasses.
To appease him the menial classes
danced to Noel Coward.

The moon fell off the squares,
leaving the island lit
by the crocodiles of wit
and the crocodiles of tears.

A treasonous joke was aimed
as he relieved himself in the garden.
Before the smiles could harden,
the dictator burst into flames.

His body went up like a flare.
As the guests turned toward him in shock,
he ignited the hollyhocks
and melted a *chargé d'affaires*.

Like a pillar of phosphorus
he burned but was not consumed.
He returned to the drawing room
grinning like Lazarus.

The attempt on his life was reported
in the opposition columns.
"Traitorous rubbish," a solemnly
weeping prime minister snorted.

The Ancient Economy

From what mercantile houses do the great
virtues descend? Capital loves its formation,
its vaults and consents, its worms of accrual

and interest. The deep breath of the treasurer
fashions from fashion some temporary profit,
mortar to bind the old flint into towers.

The ruined abbey discharges its stone
to the builder's carts, and ashlar houses
climb the castle hill. Among the arches

that acid has bitten, every chimney
has someone to brush it, every shattered boat
its crew. The presses turn their art

to artifact, and from clotted rollers come
the threaded papers of the realm.
No secret account can spoil the page

whose thin engravings buy consent:
through the fanlight of manor the colors
of new crops refract, hollow tithes

carted to the season's door. The scales
that we control, offend, false weights
gaining from each bushel a bushel,

thumb proving itself greediest of digits.
To each tomb the trial of inheritance trails,
to the privy councillor and his wife

who struck their contract with the vein of marble.
As well convict the Morgans of wrath,
the Rothschilds of murder. The blood's indentures

carry their term to term, and on their masters
levy the bargain of enclosure, the higher math
of coal. In every streak the windows catch

the bitter watchdog—hear it!—of the latch.

Political Song

Ready as weeds, corruption conspires
to catch us halfway between hall and stair
where smug little promises follow like choirs
and odors of compromise perfume the air.

Already tomorrow arrives like a truck
whose tires are flat, whose fuel pump is shot.
We're calling pure women without any luck;
we're stuck with the stock fund we shouldn't have bought.

October will blacken, November will crow,
leaving our mobsters murdered in bed
until the plea bargain descends as a low
pressure system addressed from the cops to the Feds.

When fashion returns with the gnawing of spring
and morals have changed to the whim of designers,
we'll look in the closets and not find a thing,
resign our commissions, slip out on a liner.

To the Honourable Committee

Though now the act is almost commonplace,
to beg relief from strangers courts disgrace;
but since our scholars, poets, and artistes
must worship galleries instead of priests,
it has the force of moral virtue when
it keeps the breathless arts in oxygen.
Arranged around your table in despair,
the poems can't grind coffee, carve a pear,
or make a hat rack dance like Fred Astaire.
They'll never hammer tacks through concrete blocks,
and cannot open combination locks.
Great Fannie Mae has ruled: no banker shall
accept a sonnet as collateral,
and in revenge, perhaps, for which give thanks,
the poet never reads his work in banks.
Rude politicians think it rather funny
a poet has a hard time earning money,
or if he earns a bit, and then relaxes,
the IRS will seize his sons for taxes.
Biographers are wont then to distort
impedimenta of the common sort,
for poets, like their neighbors, cannot pass
for saints or martyrs when they cut the grass.
Though verse be undercooked or overdone,
it is unread by all and bought by none,
and so within the democratic state
a poet has a democratic fate.
Because he asks foundations for largesse
who once to kings had ventured in distress,
the poet may be tempted to complain
and soothe with quarrel his distempered brain,
or play the miser, who having priced his words
reduced his speech by half, and then two-thirds.

In time it may be judged by your committee
an artist's last reserve just masks self-pity,
or that for those compression makes obscure
a weekend on the rack's the only cure.
Most honourable sirs, you must remain
as cold as snow, implacable as rain,
but spend compassionate amounts on those
whose lives were better spent in writing prose.
With your award, I'd ask leave to explore
the rundown harbors of a foreign shore
and for a year there rent a terrace house
unfrequented by *Time* or Mickey Mouse.
Like Novocain, loud supplications numb
a charity as kind as cumbersome.
If scrupulous, the poet will refine
the silence at the end of every line,
and thus, in this as elsewhere, rather throw
his voice toward whisper than fortissimo.
Good sirs, I ask approval of this grant.
With kind regards, your humble applicant.

Disease and Etiquette

Our spurious formalities will not ease
what formal lessons have not taught to bear.
The chandelier's oscillating charm

cannot charm the eye from its disease
nor entablature of cutlery exact
concession from trade unions of pain.

The sick are public property, their exposure
factors false courtesy to the science of strangers.
The scalpel in the dining room imparts

a division to the cells, from whose thin walls
procedure mends a fine, impervious modality.
What rough harlequin obliviates the empire,

whose rouged cheeks bleed like paper flowers
in the bath? Their color like a color plate
has leached the dove whose mourning rules

the actress and her agent, divine Camille's
lungs stammering to her cough like frantic wings.
The fractured call undoes the hours,

suspicion's reward comes clean to the hand:
along the carpeted hallway leading
from Bedlam to the operating theater,

antiseptic portraits guard
conventions of the dying or the lame.
How easily see evil in a wineglass,

prepare harm in a thumbprint.
Some call it plain, some garden,
where virtues or diseases harden.

· II ·

Illness in lands of plenty,
heavy-headed rye bowed to ground.
The river channel choked with slide

steams beneath weed-rendered banks.
Desert lupine purples in thunderheads.
How like virus the light,

confections of photons infecting
the breeze-struck air, thieving
our common images. Sickness breeds

possession, the throat tearing from itself
not appraisal but frail topographies.
And possession casts the body into love,

drifting down the mudded river a week
toward islands off estranged coasts.
Every weakening crews the body toward

surrender, the feverish cry
of tropical birds, purple tails
fanning like eyelashes from frondy trees,

the scratch and claw of jungle
composing diligent musics.
The sleeper of the north awakens

in the sweaty south, the jungles passed,
the ranges breached, and ahead only the shimmering
broken back of an island,

its collar of sand a proper dress for arrival.
Many, those who have visited the caves of Prospero
and returned, their suitcases never unpacked.

Shakespeare and Science

Those Roman exchanges of anatomy
        color their actors with the logic of blood,
but still the lines of inquiry encamp

strange armies on stranger hills.
        Even assassins had their theories of murder
and lived their lives as hypotheses,

not knowing how scenes beyond the walls
        of Rome would exact from them
some sacrificial allegiance

to the proscenium of friendship and farewell.
        Those who despite the fire of portent
annealing the night like a Bunsen burner

designed the dangerous experiment
        that mood and the morality of tyrants required
deserve now their retrospective autopsies

and the swarm of medical examiners.
        That all the woody world is served
by such theories as dishearten the pine

and core the oak where it stands
        sets the text upon the printer,
whose hungry hands cannot control

the accidentals that feed authority.
        What of the man who would tamper
with the exhalations of the dead?

He may tend quietly to his trials,
    willing to find what ought not be there:
the magician's island, the lover's perjured eye,

himself become at last not scientist but science.

The Virus in Rude Weather

When your body weakens toward virus
the calm enters you; familiar and slow,
like common other beauties, you devour
the products of the National Biscuit Co.

Having shaved your legs, you bathe in sunlight,
watching the wallpaper, rhododendron
by rhododendron, pretend to be dead.
You'd trade your disease with anyone.

The green-haired girls in the neighbor's garden
demand a chess notation with the real.
They don't believe disease begets desire.
What lies the world can't offer we steal,

or attempt to. Disease is cowardice, too.
Two gray squirrels mating in the attic
drown out the radio next door.
White blossoms fill the trees with static.

James at Sixty

That year, forced to purchase a garden of thorn
from the most blatant tradesman in Rye,
he built a wall to protect the half-erased landscape
beyond the wall, planning no sheep-creep or stile

that might let the other world master
the complication of this inmost port.
Days he cycled the salt flats of the Cinque Ports,
searching again for the landscape of Hawthorne,

though now America could never master
the proportions that left his felt cap awry.
The man in knickerbockers crossing a stile
into the laminated sediments of landscape

straddled a country whose landscape
failed industry, failed the sinking port
with the courage of its desolation. Style
twisted into hedgerows, a thorn

sharper than scythes measuring the rye
or gleaners who let lateness be their master.
March is a month when little left to master
bothers the impositions of landscape,

when the retreat to London or Rye
shadows a retreat to an unknown port
whose docks are rotten, gates wound with thorn.
In changing light the mind composes a style

beyond the earlier devastations of style
not even the adequate idea could master,
when if the finger were pricked with thorn
it would bleed prose into the landscape,

fill every stream with the deep red of port
and rise in the stalks of punctuation like rye.
No solitude, no desire drunk on the wry
hour by hour accretions of a style,

dictates to his typist this last report
whose every silence now welcomes its Master.
Outside, the growling dachshund cannot escape
the rope wound and wound against the red hawthorn.

The Imitative Fallacy

So complete, the imago of consciousness,

the mosquito's predatory whine
beauties itself in the clothing of childhood.
Most desire the trivial duplications,

fond schemes staring across the mattress,
grammatical children whose dependent clauses
inscribe the arc of closure. What Jamesian

revelry attaches to the intimate contrivances
events wrap themselves in, to deceive?
Blood carves its woodwork in the house of the family,

the father's sins insinuate the child's fancy,
sour oaths refuse the legal trusts.
The lizard's slow scrawl across the screen

autographs the mansion to its heirs
whose soft skin textures oak interiors.
Each child can find his father there,

the mirror's parsimonious eye
answering the spiral of its own engendering,
parent fathering parent in the incestuous

thrill of will and testament. These sheetrock
marbles testify to husbandry
in the aesthetics of regard. What inherits

is less desire than distrust, raw material
whose survival choired false successions.
It must have seemed a kind of living

could be made from alabaster.

The Duck Pond

Beneath a sky whose hardened violets
still chase a warm front's temperatures along,
the mockingbird and mourning dove await
what colder climates recognize as song.

The sluggish stream that intersects the street
is dammed for ducks, for whom its overflow
presents a danger they are pleased to skirt.
The weeds are sallow, the waterfall too low.

Reversals were our topic those weak Junes,
though then we hardly knew their harsh intent.
Along the pond, the lovers dined in twos,
pretending their dull menu would relent.

The children of the local cult had crumbed
the day's stale bread upon the water's slate.
Their parents, dressed in red, held back. A pond
erases every line its shore creates.

Distress was not a face I recognized
in yours, or mine, or any other life.
It shows how easy it was then to ignore.
Whoever saw you, saw you as a wife.

Now other things have changed. On summer nights
mosquito trucks whine back and forth in pairs,
their arcs of spray conspiring to present
blank invitations to black-tie affairs.

On the Late Murders

The inconsequence that cannot but flavor
the violence of summer afternoons
infuses the sentimental newspapers

growing slack and yellow, like old mushrooms.
Think of the rain as a curious declension
of notes, fallen from sheet music

once dryly performed. Whatever blood has been let
in dank carpeted hallways
cannot now confuse the sallow actors,

intent on the measured intonations of breathing.
On vast grids the palms are leaning
and flattering the sidewalks with fronds.

A steam rises from the walks, like steam
from battered kettles, or hot springs
where vacationing animals have gone to wallow.

The lizards stall in their shifty-eyed turning
and squadrons of dragonflies sheer the dark air,
searching for the species of their lovers

or whatever hungers can be moderated there.
An intractable fever has swollen
the thermometer's thin red vein,

and the young frog's ratchet now composes
repairs in the broken silence.
Learn to bear these soft nights

in such constructions as they allow.
The actors have withdrawn to air-conditioned rooms.
To accommodate them to philosophy

would approve the animate confusions
of their breeding, or discomfort their reading.
The nameless bug that stretches on the screen,

lounging and peculiar, like an ornament
fixed to a blouse, may seem to resent
that it, after all, has been left to direct this scene.

Haddocks' Eyes

We've received the morning post;
Royal Mail has sent a roast:
Let the ten-pound package lie
open to the blue-tailed fly.

Meat can be indifferent
with the best refrigerant
but decays within a week
and will spoil its physique.

Language functions like a sieve,
stealing what it can't forgive;
words of praise are bittersweet,
consolation indiscreet.

Soon the gosling and the goose
will attempt to reproduce,
and will pardon dead Parnell's
small affairs in grand hotels.

Politics can't save the clerk
shaken by a chance remark,
or console the cows that wait
for the slaughter by the gate,

wait for lovers to disgrace
dinner's intimate embrace
while the lakes of gravy sigh;
frozen in their boats they lie.

Famine from a satellite
won't disturb the appetite
or condemn the butcher's choice
and the methods he employs.

Diplomats soon learn to curse
border wars they can't rehearse;
generals by night confess
to their love affair with chess

and the tyrant does his part
for the sale of modern art.
In the poker game he plays
teach the losers how to raise.

Ambassador of Imperfect Mood

Close-eared specimen of the violent hour,
     species of reproach and vanity
wrapped in the unrepentant cloth
of the ministry of power,
forgive the beetle and the moth
     their reluctant Christianity.

Architect of imperfect lakes
     commanding hope of grander
prospects etched on color plates,
while through weeds the coral snake
slides, your hunger annotates
     the burned plays of Menander.

Sleeping villages will succumb
     to the grave Virgilian
virtues of your passing glance
when its martyrs have become
innocents who embrace romance,
     cold-blooded and reptilian.

The Great Wildlife of the Church

I · THE TOLERATION OF THINGS CATHOLIC

The dome of Your cathedral lists
toward wattle, where the gold leaf flakes
like elms corrupted in their social lines.
The Trappist cloisters will not trust

their issue, nor the lone investor's shrill
complaint re-arch the stony works
faith bulwarked on the plain.
The flagrant season of our neglect

virtues its tolerance past flaring eyes
in gassy audience, corrects
these outlands where the unlocked common
drains its poison to the stream, and swans

accept the spasm from its veins.
Your queues of unemployed may still regret
the loss of harrowed streets, or sidewalks whose
course of shattered brickwork implicates

the ordinary disaster of a war.
Their air accepts Your will,
as if a fin could rise from grassland,
carve a ploughman's spiral toward

the browsing horse, and Christ the shark arouse
the martyred to the dogma of the flies.
Like bowlered ravens, the faithful compose
hymns to the democrats of prose.

II · CHORALE PRELUDE

Like papal flags spread to dry the blood of heretics,
the cormorant unfolds its oilless wings.
Such affianced particulars, the bride of Christ
brokered to applause of petty dynasties,
marry vestments to the speechless village,
great coughs composed in silent rooms.
All prayer is politic, all politics prayer,
or so the statesman would console the state
with its overlay of Chartres, Charlemagne.
From such disorder can any order come—
the mad calms of snow, as who should tender
grand climates of fashion, or carve
the fungal monarchies attached to Europe's
ecclesiastic stone? The cormorant holes
the brackish backwash of these shoals.

III · *Les Très Riches Heures*

These slopes the valley's hard renewal floors
thatch dead grass with poisoned birds.
Their gray and yellow camouflage protects
        the banker's third.

The mind's unsteady instrument neglects
hilarity of conscience, but the mole
confirms the psychological caress
        and burden of its hole.

From railway platforms where we take success
to outer suburbs riddled with the flu,
the talk confuses St. Laurent with Lent
        or dollars with the Jews.

We cannot know our enemy's intent
or comprehend his kindness when the shark
creeps from the deep proportions of the sea.
        Perversion is an innocent remark,

a rude cliché made by the *maître d'*.
We do not die from it, and cannot sue
the architects whose shallow mansions offer
        no thick confronting view.

Westport after the Hurricane

Each Saturday we'd drive along the Horseneck
in our Rambler, blue as the morning sky.
Out on the horizon one stiff buoy rocked,
faithful metronome of the swell.

Pendulum of a sunken clock.
Against the beach the calm sea lapped contentedly.
In summer a few bright swimmers crawled
its flat blue board—

like a teacher's chalk marks,
her exercising scrawl of O's, O's, O's.
My father promised every week to find
the missing cottages of the rich.

He said their walls reflected pastel
colors on the sand, like our play money.
Returning from the dump, we heard
the empty moving-barrels rattle in the rear—

once one hopped off and fled
into the frozen marsh, my father in pursuit.
The beach road circled back each Saturday
to bare chimneys stripped of their pastel houses.

Methods of Empire

I · RELIGIOUS KINDLING

The ordinance of ordinary leaves,
rustle of banana turning,
incunabular insects staking their tropical claims

like bearded prospectors or, here,
the bearded oaks whose Spanish moss
houses the cliff-dwelling chiggers,

to their cost invent no theology of rank.
Into those houses the arrow of the Lord,
Whose crippled legions ferried black letter

into England, flamed the shallow rivers
and lodged in stark anatomies. The air plant
depends its species from the whole,

the whole enacts its oasis from the possible,
whose dark surrounds are desert.
And in the desert, naked and burning,

brutal strangers gather firewood and brush.
Their tall caravans assert the consequence
of trials and cities, sands whose stalks

once sprouted ranks of trees.
From the unleaved deserts messiahs hawk
their theories of the inward parts.

The violence of dry philosophies.

II · CHIAROSCURO

Such harsh slow rivers cleave a dawn
above the marsh, where reed cutters gather
a few dry sticks. The shattered call

of heron gnaws the lake's daguerreotype.
Particulars would argue a misfortune
along a shoreline raked against the mist,

whose tall aqueducts impair
proportions of the stone, and turn against the weir.
Through this landscape, steaming, raw,

three figures pass, burdened by straw panniers,
dragging a rude wheeled cart
loaded with fungal vegetables cowled like heads.

They squat among their appetites.
One cries across the lake. The heron pause,
and reed cutters turn from their blades.

Around them, gross monarchies, rotten boroughs,
a church whose silver chalice
daily chastens the vellum indulgences,

a topography festered with plague.
Such ordinary fires as on the wet sands flare
magnify the vengeance of the continent

and to what cost complicate the shore.

Sullen Weedy Lakes

was set in Palatino, a typeface designed by
Hermann Zapf. Named after Giovanbattista
Palatino, a Renaissance writing master, Palatino
was the first of Zapf's typefaces to be introduced
to America. The designs were made in 1948,
and the fonts for the complete face were
issued between 1950 and 1952.

Typeset by DEKR Corporation,
Woburn, Massachusetts. Printed and bound by
Haddon Craftsmen, Scranton, Pennsylvania.
Design by Virginia Evans.